Leena Norms is a British
Midlands. She has been s
ten years and her video e
views to date, covering everything from minimalism to
second-hand fashion to protecting the planet and surviving
your twenties. This is her first full-length collection.

Bargain Bin Rom-Com

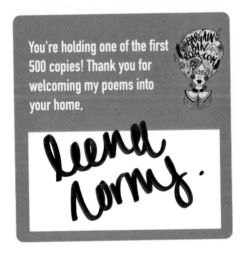

You're holding one of the first 500 copies! Thank you for welcoming my poems into your home,

Leena Norms

Leena Norms

Burning Eye

BurningEyeBooks
Never Knowingly
Mainstream

Text & Illustration Copyright © 2022 Leena Norms

This edition published by Burning Eye Books 2022

www.burningeye.co.uk

@burningeyebooks

Burning Eye Books
15 West Hill, Portishead, BS20 6LG

ISBN 978-1-913958-29-9

Cover design by Leena Norms

Bargain Bin
Rom-Com

Contents

Oh God

Oh God.
Here she goes again
with her poems –
how flickering, how
crass, this fluorescent
fucking way of
trying to make us
laugh.
I hope she doesn't ask
me if I've seen them, dayglo
and dewy – waiting for me,
served fresh each morning,
stretching over my feed like a
naked cat, a trough I'm supposed
to dive into, nose first,
guzzling up whatever
raucous revelation she
has boiled the punch out of
now. Just keep scrolling,
switch the lights off and
lie, carpet-to-face,
below the sill –
perhaps she will think
we are out.

In The Event Of Zombies

In the event of zombies
I would shut up shop with you.
Batten down the hatches,
wipe hope above the door
and wait for ruin to pass over.
I would stack cans of tuna
into a fortress and
invite you to play knights.
I would paint murals on
our ceilings until the
skies reopened,
stitch blankets
out of cancelled flights, then
kick off all the living dead when they
tried to steal our Müller Lights.
In summary, I think it's true:
I would enjoy
an apocalypse
with you.

The Librarian

Cellophane on paper grain,
he rolls the book into its cover
like a guest into a warm coat,
ready to face the outside.
Braced to collect fingerprints
like tattoos,
ready to fold her pages around their
ideas, bending in an attempt to explain,
spine strained halfway through a job.
Go get 'em, tiger! he says.
Sends her off on a trolley
to meet strangers
who will underline her good bits.

Bargain Bin Rom-Com

I kiss supermarket soliloquies into your hair,
cheap shots at your high-value heart.
Each valve is worth ten of my syllables,
but
I am duct-taping my makeshift love to you,
more *Art Attack* than artisan;
we're making it up as we go along.
A yoghurt-pot-stacked life I am hoping you will join in on,
making tunnels between years with toilet roll tubes,
holding our life goals together with PVA glue,
building towers with straws and chewing gum –
I don't know how high we will get,
but I am ready for moon-landing monologues.
One small step for us;
one giant step for the papier-mâché-held-together
love stories on earth,
designed to make Sellotape shackles rather than fasten
lovers to tandem bikes.
Up here the atmosphere is thinner
but the love feels more robust,
like if we fell back down to the world from here
we would still stand up and brush it off.

I didn't ask for Coupon Cupid to visit here.
I didn't save a pound, French franc or a mark.
All I have for you is Happy Shopper love songs,
and you offer me something like art.

Rear-View Romance

When the *I wills* turn into one *I do*,
which will one day turn into *I am*,
and all that we become will eventually drown out
all the silent things we now aren't.
All the ways we didn't.
The knots in hankies come out if you tumble
dry them enough,
issued Mr Muscle to scrub off all the ways
we were going to spend forever.
We looted our own den, spent our saved forever
on a white-veiled seatbelt.
Strange; who needs airbags if they're not going anywhere?
Who hangs rosary beads over a rear-view mirror
when the reflection will always show the inside of a garage?
I reach out my arms to catch the bouquet,
but let it sail past me;
hear it hit the floor, unclaimed.

Rachel

Rachel should have stayed on the plane.
There are dinosaurs in Paris.
I looked it up.

Greyfriars Bobby: An Intervention

Greyfriars Bobby was a dog who was well known in nineteenth-century Edinburgh for guarding the grave of his owner after he passed away. He stayed for fourteen years in total until his own death in 1872. I visited his statue many times as a child.

Bobby, Bobby, who returns to the grave,
fifty percent hero, fifty percent slave.
The loyalty of dogs and the beating hearts of men,
romanced into stone, misremembered again.

Bobby, Bobby, you'd have to be in some doubt
that a master so deep his corpse has got gout
could send nutrients up through concrete and soil,
that we could both be more than just tragically loyal.

That the call of a dead man
is louder than a field and a fire.
That love knocks and love leaves, that

skipping roll call doesn't make you a liar.
You can't hang a cap in a cemetery's hall,
or a lead. We're agreed that he'd call if
he needed a walk, but the dead don't need much;
just a visit a year still counts as 'in touch'.

You and I, we've got horizons beyond Arthur's seat!
Diplomats and poets and feral cats to meet.
Doom is a temptress, a chancer, an enslaver.
See, your blood turns to stone in service of a favour.

And company alone can't turn headstones to doors.
I'll admit I've never lived life on all fours,
but better to be free than be an obedient knave,
and life, boy, is too short to sit on a grave.

Text Back

'tb' was a common phrase used at the end of a text by teenagers in the nineties and noughties. It indicated that you'd like the recipient to reply, which sounds trite now, but (I promise) it was a salacious and vulnerable and carefully considered thing.

two little letters, *tb*: a plea to curl the words
around and send them back to me.

two little crosses, *xx*: a test to tease the
hinge behind the neck that nods a *yes*.

two little minutes, tick tick: what we did
before the read receipts that turn my throat into a brick.

two little words, *no thanks*: a way to tap,
to drain the gaps and fill the world with blanks.

Horned, Somewhere

I wonder if I am
to your friends
what you are
to mine: a horned,
winged demon,
jelly-sealed
in time; a perfectly
good partner who
sprouted teeth
overnight; a vaguely
hot ex-plus-one
who couldn't see
the light. I wonder
if we all hang
in halls of shame
somewhere, framed
by plotlines that are
showing signs of wear.
I wonder if we
button up what
otherwise would spill
out: that villains relay
victories when they
get to pick the route.

The Divorce

To add any weight to his disgrace
there must be some handprint on her face,
some lipstick on a collar in some forgotten drawer,
some white skin where a ring must have been before.
Some *Something* to make a rubbing of,
a body to trace, a very shocking *Something*
to waltz in and replace:
the way he greets us at parties;
the ten minutes a week in which we exchange pleasantries;
the time he bought a round, recommended
us a Great Little Place; the way
he looked at her as he drew her down the aisle
with his eyes. The day he took us by
surprise by doing the bare minimum, knighted
by our easy enthusiasm and the sinking
feeling that there are no good ones left, anyway.
Until then we leave her in the doorway, doubtful
as to whether she really needs a room at the inn.
Unsure now, in the absence of a handprint,
we'd know where to begin.

Hiraeth

I don't know if you've ever crept up on a memory
and slid plastic over its head, but
home is a place in a Ziploc bag I carry
around and wave in the faces of strangers;
tilt it to the light to demonstrate its superior
edges, all the ways the sharp parts
add character, pizzazz, grit.
Then, lightly, tip it back to properly showcase
the hanging baskets, the steaming Sunday roasts;
make sure I walk you around the
circumference,
inhale your *ahhs* and *oohs*
as I perfectly demonstrate all the ways
the atrium of my faults is simply
architecture in disguise.

Lovebites In Lockdown

Today I woke with hair full of
glycerine and glitter
to a flat that is not a flat
but a snowglobe.
Something to shake up, but not out of.
Doors fading through
disuse, like dew,
and windows becoming paintings of what
the world could look like today:
unprovable.

Verification Application

Okay, you got me.
I want an icky blue tick,
a quickie blue tick;
however much I hate it,
I want a sickly blue tick.
A blue tick to make the
sands quick, to pass the
grains through the glands,
CLICK! See? You've got your
palms on my life's joystick;
they'll think I'm thick
until I've got a blue tick.
You think I can pick who
gets the tick? I'm a list
of checkboxes waiting to
twirl and high-kick! *PLEASE,*
I just need this lick;
it's like I've got a neck crick,
feeling so unmoored it's
making me seasick. After all...
it's not like I'm asymmetric –
plus I have *FOUR* photos that
have more likes than the girl
with legs like broomsticks.
This verification form is
JURASSIC and I am
the last known survivor of
this *TITANIC* depravity, this
modern daylight calamity;
this industrial tick complex is

so acidic I'm positively balsamic.
Please, it's just a cerulean tick,
just tacky enough
to make the fame stick. I wish,
as I'm sure you do, that we lived
in a post-tick age of polyphonic perfection,
but for now I'll just take the tick,
if you have no objection?

Test Me!

Lead on, down stark stocked shelving
aisles, lead me like a bride to the
mortar, the dirty danger of dented
powders, rows of raucous rouge and
sticky serotonin sold in shades like
deep-throat, dare, nestle, bud, bare.
The pucker of mascara as you pop the head
from its sheath, the sneaky flick of sealed pots
to see what's underneath. How I long
to plunge chipped fingers into blush putty,
twist lipstick bullets to climax and
burrow face-first into the syrups of cells
and mucus and femme fatale fluids, the
debris of sister-strangers in debit
  card delight,
until my toes curl like old
  receipts and I realise:

That's probably how I got all those colds, right?

Some Days

Some days it's hard to believe
that people want more from you
than simply their own beliefs
repeated back to them, a
potato-print mirror of their own
top drawer, assembled in another
workshop entirely, made from unfamiliar
material, designed to solve
a completely different anxiety.
Working in suede when you've
been moulding polystyrene,
setting theirs in stone while
you set yours with a firing.
But in my pocket I keep a test tube,
a secret belief that what they
really want to hear
is
that they are not *bad*,
even though they may be *wrong*.
That they aren't *done* for,
even though so much is lost.
That when they die
all isn't gone, because they were not *all*,
and that set-jaw sweetness
outlives us, despite ourselves.

Twelve Ways To Skin A Dream

1.   Roll it over, spread its legs,
         start at the chin and let everyone in.

2.   Start at the spine, twist its limbs,
         curl it around trellis,
         let it meander towards the sky.

3.   Tell everyone that you are besotted, hoping it will hear,
         but snub its clumped-mascara fluttered proposition.

4.   Leave it at the bottom of a wash basket
         until it asserts its dominance,
         stinks out your office shirts
         and lets everyone know what you only
         guess at.

5.   Exfoliate it until you see bone,
         watch its marrow spiral down the drain
         in ringlets.

6.   Give it forms and a biro,
         let it fester in the waiting room amongst
         the magazines,
         the last to be seen.

7.   Copyright strike it until it feels
         like a shadow, or a lost boy
         at a window.

8.   Tax it for staying, for growing, for shrinking.

9.   Make it look silly in a jokeshop hat,
       mock it behind its back.

10.   Put a ring on it and let it see you with other people.
       Come home late, smelling of mortgage,
       someone else's wishes on your collar.
       Only touch its waist at parties
       or hold it so tight you crack its ribs.

11.   Cover it in your lipstick
       and never call again.

12.   Pay someone to teach you how to touch it, but
       never ask it what it wants.

Bargaining With The Photocopier

I am elbow-deep in the teeth of
a plastic beast, wrestling for paper
I don't even want, bargaining with her in
hushed tones to return me to
the place where knuckles are for
dragging and not for white-knuckle
rides through Q2 meetings about
unmet KPIs and trinket swapping.
How much, I say, *for you to*
release me back to the forest?
Call her to come and get me,
let me perch on a branch until
she picks me up. There has been some
mistake; I should be stooping
below skies of pitch and humming
in a key that doesn't have a name yet.
Return me to myself, hairy and
bedraggled, full of splinters and hard skin,
unpainted toenails pressed into
thick marshes, belly to the clouds as
I howl at a full inbox in the sky,
willing it to leave me down here.
I ask the beast if she knows I am
an outdoor cat, if she knows where the flap
to the garden is, how to end this loop of
litter tray to laminator to litter tray again,
how to stop the angry letters coming:
all the demands for paper like the stuff
she eats and spits, as if photocopying
is her hobby and not her full-time gig.

How do you do it? I say. *Withdraw your
weight and still get treated like you're pulling?*
Petal, she croaks from behind her
eyelashes, *is this your first day
in the jungle?*

Bad News Square

A 'found' poem from my news feed.

At least 22 people killed after
some people compare Boris Johnson to a
luxury sale at criminal prices, available while
child stars that have aged like fine wine
suffer fatal injuries from a fairground's worst
glamorous prime minister, 36.
Ash cloud sends people sprinting from
giant Christmas jumper retailing at £30,000.
Mortician shares opinion on dead
Tinder date who called me chubby and talked to me about
corgis, who were compared to bunnies as they hop through
misogynistic tropes that have to be stopped.
Two feet of snow as Met Office warns heavy
flow was lighter than usual when using experimental
kindness, as mum thanks man who offered new space for her
late son's memorial garden. Survival
doubtful, but Oscar nomination likely
for life on Planet Earth.

Meet Commute

My heroes are dead,
my enemies are in power,
and still I must brave the shower,
brave the pavement,
brave the bus,
brave the slipping, sour *us*,
dig among the putrid bins,
dust off hope
and still give it keys,
still let it live here,
let it breathe.

Ark

I drag parts of myself
out onto the drive,

all the spare wood
I can muster

from the depths of
a garage bunker,

stocked by a father
who fears only

an apocalypse where
we have ample food

but B&Q is closed. Two
planks at a time until

Malcom from 49 asks,
arms crossed, what

I am up to, and I tell him
that I am up to my eyes

in rising doom and an
ark is in order. His Jill

joins him, and Mrs Davies
from 47, and soon they

are all watching me
assemble something that

could be a raft or more
likely a toboggan. Night

falls and my audience
disperse, except Mrs

Davies, who reappears
with a steaming mug

which she places on the
driveway and requests that,

if we are to march in two
by two, she will not have

to bring her husband.

Pantry For A Slipping World

In my pantry
I keep ten cans of tuna.
One bottle of pop from a newsagent's long closed,
a pillowcase strewn with worn brown delilahs
in case I want to lay my head in my childhood
bedroom again.
Four stamped, addressed envelopes
to relatives long dead.
Five hardback classics
for a fictional future
in which I will be well-read.
Clean water – two-gallon bottles
for when they up the price of life.
A crown of daisies
pushed up by ancestors
I never played chess with.
A Walkman and
a half-unravelled tape of the world news
the day he died,
so I can hear all the ways the world
was good that day.
A sleeping bag
with Galway grass still stuck to it,
a stray Queen of Spades at the bottom
from late-night tent games.
Coffee grounds in a large jar
preserved like a body part:
a naïve display of all the productivity
yet to come.
Two dried-up nail polish pots from

sleepovers time forgot.
A stray pen with five nibs,
colours that click into place,
so I can write the rainbow
and my own promise
never to drown myself again.
A matchbox filled with teeth
and a childish belief
that I will never need
any of this.

The Reward For Excellence Can No Longer Be Money

The reward for excellence
can no longer be money.
Perhaps I can interest you
in a bag of glitter? Or
a small litter of adoring puppies? We
can include bows on their collars
at no extra cost. Free rein in a garden
of bluebells? A puzzle with the last piece ready
to pop in? A walking tour of all your favourite
sunsets against all your favourite skylines? If you'd like
to never work again
that can be arranged, although activities
are recommended to keep you from the brain abyss,
and we must warn you that most people end up doing
something
despite themselves. Oh, and:
Congratulations! You are excellent at something!
Really! Truly! Excellent! Is that
what you wanted to hear? Is that what you
have been sticking your neck out for?
If you'd rather a yacht we can
arrange for you to borrow one from the boat library? Only
perhaps you could wait
on the request for a champagne bath until we
have sorted the clean drinking water? Unless, of course,
as our resident excellence, you have any ideas about that?

. . .

No worries! Thank you for
understanding; you are taking this
very well. And, now that the reward for excellence can
no longer be money, we're excited to hear
what you will demand instead.

What A Wonderful Way To Go

What a wonderful way to go,
that we loved the world too much to speak of its going,
and us with it, ravelled up in each other;
the daily fireworks of lunch boxes lost
and long fights about tea towels, talk of
apocalypse mislaid among the school trip
forms and well-thumbed books about
star-crossed dramas between two small
skeletons who only wished for the other to live.

What a wonderful way to go,
the kind of denial that has a tenderness to it.
Let the future dead plains know that we
were too vigorously wrapped up
in each other to look up at the sky
and notice the damp spots there,
for when you are in love you don't have time
to spare to hark to landlords about
light fittings. There will always be time.

What a wonderful way to go,
and awful too; the lavish child who launches
rockets while bodies writhe in the streets,
and fingerpaints forevers onto crumbling
walls; the way we crown the five people
closest to our face and forget the rest.
And so the moon blinks, disappointed
but not surprised, leaves through the back door,
hoping his next stop will really last.

Beer Garden In Three Degrees Of Warming

Picket fences and double-glazed forevers
flutter in your stomach, less turned
than mine, and I, out of politeness,
offer up my preference: *a two-bed*
with a view, a chance to drive to B&Q
and fight over things like sea green or
cappuccino cream, delicious California citron
behind a frame wall, an oak kitchen
door that leads to decking that—

I blink to crash the waves behind
my eyelids, puce and rising, full
of farmed-salmon ceiling tiles,
and I say,

Sure, the second bedroom could
be a study, you're right, whilst mentally
converting it into a larder
of tin cans and ion battery packs,
wondering if the estate agent will mind me
bringing a trowel to viewings, just
to turn the soil and test it for hope,
or, better yet, the ground beneath it;
see if it's soft enough to dig to the centre
and carve out our little piece of now,
snap it from the motherland and float
upwards instead of sideways, ripping
us and all our sacred belongings
from the rotting elements and
the curse of context to forge a limp tomorrow

for just a
few more days
breathing.
Clink.

You tap my glass. *Another?*

Sure.
And I sink back into a bed of blackout blinds,
fuchsia futon fantasies and houseplants
that will not grow to swallow us, and wonder
who will be there to collect the mortgage.

Off The Edge

Get off the grass.
around square inches
Or would you have
inches from lawns
Would you have me
wait there like a
I have enough nuts to
door bolting rights? I
they were unhooking
from the wall, that
or in gilded two-beds.
a welcome that never was?
the first place, wouldn't
assigned me a square to
to tap-dance my first steps
dimensional?
I am an idea
theory to pursue, and not
suppose we charge for
remember the first
over my mum's
indignant, the drip, drip,
plopped and I learnt
and pouring into moats,
bridges and cliffs:
damned

Must I build a moat
  to exist upon?
  me hover, like a board,
and lavish patios?
  climb a tree and
  hoarding squirrel until
  swap for nuts and
  learnt long ago, when
my father's six-inch screen
you can squat in gutters
  Tell me, can I outstay
    If I was welcome in
      they, upon my birth, have
      stand on? A teensy ten inches
    across? Am I not three-
  Or perhaps
    to you, and 'home' just a
    air or *water*, although I
    matter, don't we? I
  Severn Trent bill I read
  shoulder and being
    drip before the penny
    that water was for selling
why people jump from
dead if they sink,
if they float.

If This Poem Wasn't A Poem

If this poem wasn't a poem, it would be:
A to-do list.
A performance assessment.
A way to tell myself to do more,
faster.
A failed attempt to stave off
disaster.
An invisibility cloak
to disappear into.
A piece of music
to drink gin to.
A getaway car.
A flatpack box.
A face-lifter
without Botox.
A crate of dreams
wrapped in ticking dynamite.
Two hundred and seventeen attempts
to get it right.

Small Talk

Ask me what I remember most about my grandad.
Which coastline I always have one foot planted on.
Whose hand I can still feel on my palm if I leave it out of a pocket.
If I only call my friends in the kind of emergency I can articulate.
If it comforts me that my chosen candidate in the 2062 election
    has not been born yet.
Ask me who I am when I'm alone and if I can mimic it for you.
If I dog-ear pages of holy books I no longer live by because I still
    need to know where I came from.
Ask me which building my blue plaque would be nailed to,
or if it hurts when I pluck my eyebrows, if it hurts when I leave
    the house, if it hurts when I don't leave the house, if it hurts
    to have a house at all.
Ask me if at some point I'll get a husband just because I've lost
    all my best friends to theirs.
Ask me if I used to get jealous watching the boys play football so
    freely on the tarmac.
Ask me if I only picked up a book in the first place so I could
    raise it across my gaze to block out all the ways I wasn't
    allowed to run.
Ask me if there are people I've lost who I'm still holding
    auditions to replace,
whom I would give up a career to help die,
if I ever lose hope or if I hang it on a keychain by the door at
    night so I can get to it in an emergency.
Ask me what the best lipstick for a broken heart is (I know that
    one).
Ask me what the last book I dropped in the bath was,
who the Prime Minister was when I was born,
how I say no to the things I don't want to do.

Ask me who blocks out the holes in my heart when they
    curl themself around me.
Ask me if you can curl yourself around me.
I will say no,
but at least you know more about me now than 'how I am'.

Two-Point-Oh

For my grandmother, who was also named Kathleen Normington.

We have never met, but
I have your name, first and last,
your round features,
your metabolism.
I wish I could show you
all the ways I get to be a person now.
That this Kathleen
gets hopes and dreams
and a chance to own herself.
That we get a voice
in the next round;
that the world gets kinder
when the second edition comes out.

Surname

I hover over
Surname:
and a knot in me crackles,
a fire pit at the bottom still
glowing, smudged dust of all
the names hoarded below my
floorboards: Doyle, Walsh,
Apthomas, Griffin, Crow, Cook, Hughes.
Never considered for repetition,
inked over as the bells
swing, puffed out in a
flurry of confetti, the bobbing
heads of women I never knew,
like ducks hooked at a fête,
floating to my surface,
rolling their eyes and
shaking their aprons
at me, shrugging as if
to say:
I never liked it anyway
and half meaning it.
I open my mouth to ask
to be reminded of my name
and a smoke ring
rises out, forms a crop circle before
floating out of the window,
conspiratorially hissing
under her breath.

The Three Apparitions Of Luxury

I met Luxury on a Wednesday,
drinking rosé bubbles in a speakeasy,
gold earrings tickling her collarbone.
I met Luxury and she pulled my wrist
through dance halls and discos and living rooms filled with light.
I met Luxury and we talked all through the night.
I met Luxury and she twisted jokes through my ears in French,
painted my nails the colour of money,
laughed kindly at my accent,
planted bulbs around my frame.
Luxury always reminded me of her name.

Later, I would meet Luxury at a gig;
she'd dip-dyed her life in cheaper fabric.
Luxury wore brogues and spoke in beat poetry.
She pulled me by the elbow through
boat parties and bright parks,
pressed philosophy through my palms in the dark.
Luxury served sourdough on crumpled duvets,
taught me to trick landlords and open ISAs,
only let her brow crease on weekdays,
remembered to point to her fire escapes
and the envelopes beneath her floorboards.

The last time I saw Luxury, she had moved home.
The down without the out, Luxury had lost
everything but her books and two big-hearted
boomers who welcomed her back to an untouched
attic room with a router and a skylight. Her dead ringer heroines,
still plastered over peeling wallpaper,

watched over her as she resketched the floor plans of herself.
And though Luxury gathers nicknames,
moves house, switches lives, pours coffee or champagne,
I know I will know Luxury
when I see her again.

Saturday At A National Trust

Padding around flagstone hallways
laid by peeling hands,
wallpaper wilting to show
its hand,
the scribbled beliefs
not printed on the handouts.
A redraft of a world half built
before crumbling.
Melted minutes
into candles burning low
so as not to spotlight
what sits in dark corners
watching.
Paint licks over a coat of arms
to honour the merchants
that are pirates in another tongue.
If you sit in the ladies'
– quiet –
you can hear the women wailing
through the paintwork.

New Mantras For Future Fridge Magnets

I honour my ancestors by becoming their opposite.
Just because there is not blood on my hands
does not mean there is not blood underneath my
fingernails.

I honour my ex by leaving my heart on the latch.
A well-timed taxi home after a party is not a tragedy;
it is the best passed Post-it note for avoiding living out
a trope.

I honour my work by not bleeding its lines.
Not sticking an IV in it when it isn't supposed to live,
letting it sustain me without giving it a vein
to drink from.

I honour my friends by giving our friendship new
names, new and specific ways to say, *I promise*,
I will, I'll only leave you if you
need me to.

Repeat Performance

When the water beats on
June windows, I feel the
wriggle in my bones.
It's the beat beat beat of
a bumbled defiance, a way
for summer to say, *I*
am more than a season,
you know. I can bleed
like
the rest of them;
I
can be spontaneous too.
Just because a girl burns
a back does not mean
she can't return with a
bucket, or feel remorse.
Just because you've seen me
before does not mean
you should count on me
again.

Thirty

Time clears her throat
and grumbles to see me pass
another of her notches
giving in to faff…
But faff is sweet and faff is dirty,
faff keeps me up with flirting,
faff stops the boards from skirting
and the pictures from hanging
themselves on Farrow & Ball walls
in curling cul-de-sacs
that burn like paper inside books
that really could have been something
had they not wanted to be too warm.
Cosy kills, I mutter, and let the
faff flutter me for another forty
filthy minutes. *Take that, Time*, I say.
And she rolls her eyes and vows
to smudge my tattoos for that.

Unclean Magdalene

As if it wasn't enough
to be without a railcard,
apparently now I have to
embalm myself, nightly,
like some kind of Egyptian
ruler. Except it's just me
and the jars in a stare-off
because I am, I hear,
inherently dirty and clogged,
and so I fight gunk with gunk
and put myself to eternal rest,
singing prayers of absolution
over my superfood face oil,
then sprinkling holy toner,
then carrot-infused eye cream
before I can consider ordering
an aspergillum off Amazon
to hasten the retinol revolution.
Fourteen stations of the skin
for the sin of not living in a placid
state on a spinning ball of fire
in a volatile and cruel galaxy,
or at least arranging my face
like none of it is happening.

As It Turns Out

I am delighted to declare
that no one is watching.
Not as you pull on your coat
awkwardly, elbows touching
behind your back like a small
dinosaur.
Not as you push the 'pull', screw
the pop-top, retrace your steps to
track your own shadow down.
No one is watching while you
wiggle through turnstiles a little
more snugly than the previous
week. No one is counting
your cookies on their voyage
from packet to mouth, or the times you have
to wipe your glasses on your jumper.
No one notices when you slip
back through the shop
to retrieve that *one* ingredient
you always forget; the world
is not rolling its eyes to the back
of its head every time you
forget to charge your phone
or call home or water that plant
that only you pass. No one is
counting like you, clouting
like you. There is
no abacus of your miniature
discrepancies mounted on
a spike somewhere, nor an

enchanted loom spinning
a report card on your life while
hurtling towards an
end point that is large enough to
swallow you but narrow enough to
spit you back out for not wearing
the right shoes or bringing the right
set of keys.
And as we spin on this relatively
dull and at once brilliant rock, as we
hurtle through a dark wardrobe filled
with pricks of light and downright
thoughtless pricks to accompany them,
what a relief to no longer feel witnessed;
to lick a finger and scoop yesterday's
crumbs from the counter without
damnation.

Sundae

We sit on two sides of the same sundae,
pull different ends of the same spaghetti
through our teeth.
Almost romance,
not quite a success,
our two appetites
baked together
and broken like bread.
One suffocating, the other one
never full.
We are icing, piping through the day,
laying the groundwork
for a numbing
sticky toffee tomorrow
never coming,
and then arriving
all at once.
And there are hundreds of thousands
of reasons
to turn away
from myself,
but we lick the same lid
and lie in the same bed,
her: snoring, satisfied.
Me: asking the ceiling
for better ways
to fill a life.

Mum's A Word

Mum is a word
drizzled over cornflakes and handed to you
on your way to the day.
A folded pile of useful words left on the stairs
to use when you need them.
It's yet another drive to drop off
yet
another
gym kit. It's a letter written to 'the adults'
in your defence. It's a *no-because-I-love-you,*
a yes, bring your friends, I made
a bed up for them too. It's an *I won't always*
agree, but I'll make you a sandwich to eat on your way.
Mum is a person who teaches you
that Mum is not a person at all,
but a note slipped under a door that says,
Everyone deserves this.

Lesser-Known Love Languages

The forgiven drip of tea
on new cushions, untotted
and dismissed with a toffee wink.
An open biscuit tin wedged between
knees, rather than carefully counted
out on allocated crockery.
The dip of a chin that
nods you through when it
isn't your turn, the extra pen slid
across the desk, the tripped name
on the tip of your tongue, offered
before the beat that would have
made it awkward. The
heads-up that there's *no loo
roll in that one*, the hands that hold
heavy doors and wave you across
roads, oceans, days.
The little ways we pass the note that
says
you exist
in all the teensiest, trivial ways.

When They Switch The Sky Back On

A response to 'Yellow' by Anne Sexton.

When they turn the sky
on again, we will forget
it was ever off.
Forget we cowered under the
ghosts of trees we did not plant,
rallies we never got around to.
We will forget how we wandered around
writing signatures on each other,
petitioning ourselves into being,
sandbags of legislation
finally appearing
now the court is closed.
We will drain parliament,
dry it out like laundry,
wipe the tidelines off the walls
and pretend, as if to a supply teacher,
that *we never saw*
nothing; and we'd be right.
When they turn the sky on again
we will, for the first time,
know it is there
and bury the switch, forever.

Always One

There is always one
and it might as well be
you: the one who eats the last
biscuit, fails to read the room,
buries her to-file pile in a private
tomb. There is always one,
and rarely two, who adds
an asterisk to a perfect view.
Who won't cough up the time, spends
it pushing dust around her
plate, adjusting hair,
counting chickpeas, dribbling
honey on countertops,
leaving the world a little
tackier, grubbier, creasing
just-made beds, missing
calls and trains, not
getting what the fuss is,
not getting out enough, not
staying in enough. There's
always one, and it's your turn
to let the world burn
a little. Just a smoulder, to
not always have to be the one
to have wet tea towels on hand,
to let the ball drop, be watched
by others, to admit you haven't
seen it and don't intend to.
Set the plates to simply turn,
confess to apathy, or at least

a delicious taste for tinkering,
faffing and not finishing
everything with a bow, and do
it all with your baggage in tow.
Buy an extra seat, spread out.
Let them move and reroute.
Be the one who repeats a bad performance
without clearing her dressing room,
sticks the lashes on harder
this time, holds the baby awkwardly,
makes the wrong joke, fucks up
in the frying pan but passes them off as
'smoked'.
There is always one; it's nothing new.
There's always one, and it might as well
be you.

Make Art For Your Friends

Make art for your friends
because when the world bends back on itself
every heart will need art tailor-made for them.
The Band-Aids of big hits won't fit.
It will be close-knit nitwits
who will keep each other from burning
and rather draw them around a fireside,
because when they cut the phone lines,
shut off the Wi-Fi,
it will be you who will have to assemble the hope.
No flatpacks now;
you will need to score the pattern from scratch,
carving jokes that match the misfortune,
whittling wisdom from broken beams
and speaking dreams where the memes once were.
You are the raw material the next teenagers have been
waiting for.
When love is relocalised it won't matter if your work has
    been 'done' or revised;
there is still something special about a bad panto in a
    draughty hall
when the postcode is your own.
There is still hope in the handwriting that refuses to be
    mass-produced for the world.
And the world will be so silent – and so chatty all at once.
Like a reunion at the back of the bus
between friends who have been behind screens for too long
and found eleventh-hour love songs
to sing in the storm.

Silent Night

You do not have to give everything.
You can keep a sock for yourself.
Pin it to the mantelpiece,
fill it with everything you've missed:
baths and books and blood-red confessions
of how you really felt this year.
The secret sweet wrappers and swear words,
the time you pretended to answer the question you hadn't
heard,
the nails you stepped on and the replies
you didn't get around to.
You do not have to leave milk for a man
who only visits when it suits,
or carrots for his friends; keep the cookies,
light the fire, let it lock your house.
Feel the silence as a wealth;
keep a bit of merriness for yourself.

[the sound of ripping paper]

This is your permission slip
to leave.
To care more than is normal,
although it is less than is needed.
To absolutely not be over it.
To have been over it before
it even happened.
To clear some floorspace and
begin again amid the rot,
to place a bet on your
own tired horse, your own
flailing brain, your two
dimpled legs. To live in amicable
apathy with your body,
like a worn-in couple
who forget their anniversary.
To wait for *the thing*. You
know? The *thing*. The *thing*
you are always waiting for,
but to find some joy while you do.
To decorate the waiting room in
bright colours and bring your
favourite flask; to assemble
a playlist and stick it in the ears
of whoever passes through.
To select the soundtrack
even when you cannot pick
the plot. This is your permission
slip, so if anyone tries to stop you
slipping out in the night
to the airport, they won't be able
to keep you from the sky.

Acknowledgements

The real heroes of this poetry collection are the librarians of Coventry and Warwickshire, who lent me my very first poetry books, gave me space to read them and now, two decades later, let me use their big sprawling tables to assemble this collection, their scanners to scan in my illustrations and their printers to provide proof copies. Long live libraries everywhere.

To the women who cheered my little poetry heart on, beta-read, prodded, praised and rooted for my writing even when I didn't: Sara, Erin, Mia, Hannah, Clarissa, Kat.

To the Gumption Club for giving me everyday oomph, time to write and proof that people on the internet are nice, really.

To the Burning Eye team, who read *Doom Rolled in Glitter* and essentially went 'MORE PLEASE!' – thank you for everything.

Most of all, to Craig, who is my first reader, graphic design first-aider, prize-winning pep-talker, top rom-com dish and best friend.